AR 4.6 | 0.5

S0-BHX-516

Mix It Up!
Solution or Mixture?

by Tracy Nelson Maurer

Science Content Editor:
Shirley Duke

Rourke
Educational Media

rourkeeducationalmedia.com

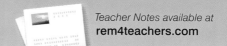

Teacher Notes available at
rem4teachers.com

Science Content Editor: Shirley Duke holds a bachelor's degree in biology and a master's degree in education from Austin College in Sherman, Texas. She taught science in Texas at all levels for twenty-five years before starting to write for children. Her science books include *You Can't Wear These Genes, Infections, Infestations, and Diseases, Enterprise STEM, Forces and Motion at Work, Environmental Disasters,* and *Gases.* She continues writing science books and also works as a science content editor.

www.rourkeeducationalmedia.com

Photo credits: Cover © Mikeledray, Paskomaksim; Pages 2/3 © Denis Tabler; Pages 4/5 © Andrjuss, ILYA AKINSHIN, violetkaipa, Aaron Amat; Pages 6/7 © Torian, Neveshkin Nikolay, JustASC, Charlotte Lake, photosync, Pakhnyushcha, kedrov, R-photos, ; Pages 8/9 © violetkaipa, Vlad Siaber, CAN BALCIOGLU; Pages 10/11 © Krupicki, Lightspring, WM_idea, Leigh Prather, joingate; Pages 12/13 © windu, Kokhanchikov, Tarasyuk Igor, Quayside; Pages 14/15 © Stephen Firmender, JeremyRichards, Denis Tabler; Pages 16/17 © ivosar, Subbotina Anna; Pages 18/19 © Carolina K. Smith, M.D., AISPIX by Image Source; Pages 20/21 © fotohunter, AISPIX by Image Source

Editor: Kelli Hicks

My Science Library series produced by Blue Door Publishing, Florida for Rourke Educational Media.

Library of Congress PCN Data

Maurer, Tracy Nelson
 Mix It Up! Solution or Mixture? / Tracy Nelson Maurer
   p. cm. -- (My Science Library)
 ISBN 978-1-61810-094-8 (Hard cover) (alk. paper)
 ISBN 978-1-61810-227-0 (Soft cover)
 Library of Congress Control Number: 2012930295

Rourke Educational Media
Printed in the United States of America,
North Mankato, Minnesota

rourkeeducationalmedia.com

customerservice@rourkeeducationalmedia.com • PO Box 643328 Vero Beach, Florida 32964

Table of Contents

All Mixed Up!

Why do some ingredients seem to disappear when you mix them together? Why don't others? Here's the scoop on mixtures and solutions!

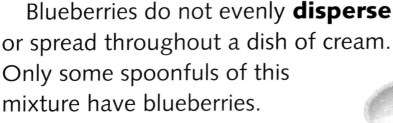

Blueberries do not evenly **disperse** or spread throughout a dish of cream. Only some spoonfuls of this mixture have blueberries.

Sugar stirred into water makes a solution. The sugar seems to disappear, or **dissolve**, because it disperses evenly through the water.

Sand does not dissolve when stirred into water. This is a mixture. A mixture is a combination of at least two substances, with different properties, that don't chemically combine. The materials in a mixture can be separated. A solution is a special mixture in which one thing dissolves in another, making a single form. The materials don't separate.

Try This:

Add one teaspoon of salt to a cup of water in a clear glass. Stir the salt. Did the salt seem to disappear? Is this a solution or a mixture? How do you know?

Mixtures and solutions exist everywhere: foods, medicines, plastics, and building products. They're even inside of you! Digestion, for example, ends with waste leaving your body as feces (mixture) or urine (solution).

Examples of mixtures:

concrete with pebbles

glitter nail polish

trail mix

cookie dough

Sticky Notes

In 1968, a scientist at 3M tried to invent airplane glue. The solution wasn't sticky enough. A co-worker later used the tacky solution to make a removable bookmark. Eureka! Sticky notes!

Examples of solutions:

tea

perfume

rubber cement

cough syrup

What State Is It In?

liquid

solid

Water, a liquid, cooled to 32° Fahrenheit (0° Celsius) turns into a solid. Heated until it boils, water turns into a gas called water **vapor**.

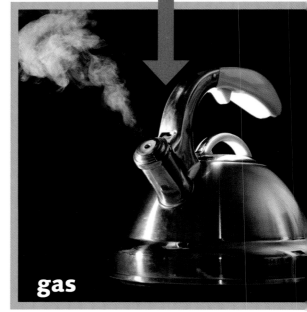

gas

Some materials mix easily. Others won't mix at all. It depends on the tiny moving particles in matter called **molecules** that define its **physical properties**, including its state. Almost everything on Earth exists in one of three states: solid, liquid, or gas.

molecule

State Discoveries

Matter may exist in at least two additional states, such as Bose-Einstein condensates or plasmas. Understanding plasmas helped create flat screen televisions.

Solids have a definite shape. Their packed molecules move very little.

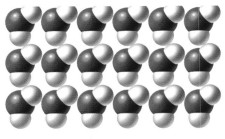

Packed molecules in a solid move slowly.

Liquids take the shapes of their containers.

Out of containers, liquids flow because their molecules have room to slip under and over each other.

Gases do not have shapes unless they are in containers. Then their molecules bounce off the container walls and completely fill the containers.

Making Physical Mixtures

Mixtures combine materials from at least two of the three main states.

Solid + Solid

One way to create a physical mixture is to mix a solid with another solid. Decayed plants or animals and stones mix to make soil.

Fact Focus:
Wiggling earthworms help stir the soil mixture.

Liquid + Solid

A liquid with a solid can make a mixture. Milk is a mixture of liquid water, fat, and milk solids.

Fact Focus: Generally, mixtures do not look clear because the solids in them block the light. Most solutions appear clear when the solids dissolve. Nothing remains to block the light.

Liquid + Liquid

Adding two liquids together can make a mixture. Vinegar and vegetable oil mix briefly when shaken to make salad dressing. Yum!

Liquid + Gas

A liquid with a gas can make a mixture. Liquid soap mixes with tiny bubbles of gas and puffs into foam.

Gas + Solid

A gas with a solid can make a mixture. Soot, solid flecks of burned material, mixes with hot air to make smoke.

Bubbly Science

In the 1770s, English scholar Joseph Priestley lived near a brewery where he studied beer bubbles. He learned how to mix **carbon dioxide** gas under pressure with water to make sparkling water. Soda pop began with Priestley's chemistry work!

Joseph Priestley

Stirring Solutions

The receiving substance of a solution is called a **solvent**. The liquid, solid, or gas that mixes into the solvent is called the **solute**.

Gas + Liquid

Adding a gas to a liquid can make a solution. Oxygen from air dissolves in water. Fish use their gills to capture the oxygen molecules.

Solid + Liquid

Adding a solid to a liquid can make a solution. Instant coffee crystals stirred into hot water melt into coffee.

Fact Focus: Water is the most common solvent on Earth.

Liquid + Liquid

Scientists experiment with solutions every day. They recently developed an important solution using two liquids. E85 is a blend of **ethanol** made from corn oil and gasoline.

Many drivers use ethanol in their vehicles, because the corn in this fuel is a renewable resource.

Can you make a solution? Here's one way. A glass of milk is the solvent. Blow into the milk with a straw. You are putting carbon dioxide gas into the milk. That's the solute. Bubbles form in your solution. Can you make another solution?

When you blow bubbles in milk through a straw, that's a gas plus liquid solution. Add chocolate to the milk, and you'll make another solution!

Inventing a mixture or a solution, such as E85, often raises important questions. What does it cost to make? Does it help or hurt the planet? Who can use it?

Scientists continue to experiment with mixtures for fuels, such as biodiesels made from vegetable oils.

Every new mixture or solution is an opportunity to discover more about the world and ourselves.

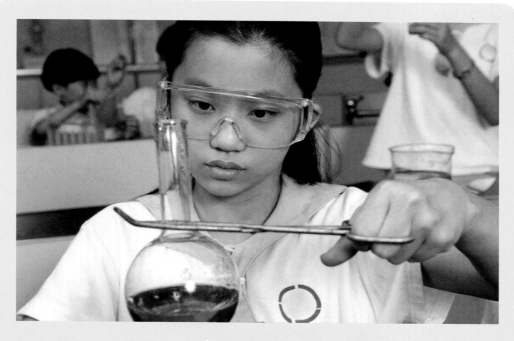

Safety First!

Before experimenting with any mixtures, ask an adult to help. Check that the mixtures do not explode or produce toxic fumes. Wear safety glasses and follow instructions carefully.

Show What You Know

1. What other mixtures can you think of?

2. What other solutions do you know?

3. Imagine you invented a new solution. What does it do? Why?

Glossary

carbon dioxide (KAR-buhn dye-AHK-side): a colorless gas produced by plants, exhaled by humans, and released by some burning materials

disperse (diss-PURS): to scatter or spread apart

dissolve (di-ZAHLV): to seem to disappear into another substance

ethanol (ETH-uh-nahl): a colorless liquid made from corn that can burn

molecules (MAH-luh-kyoolz): the smallest bits of a substance that retain all the characteristics of the substance; a combination of like or different atoms

physical properties (FIZ-i-kuhl PRAH-pur-teez): qualities or traits of something

solute (SAHL-yoot): the substance that dissolves in solvent

solvent (SAHL-vuhnt): a substance that can dissolve one or more other substances

vapor (VAY-pur): very tiny particles of water that are visible as they hang in the air

Index

Websites to Visit

www.chem4kids.com

http://climate.nasa.gov/kids/

www.sciencenewsforkids.org

About the Author

Tracy Nelson Maurer likes science experiments, especially the cooking kind! She lives in Minnesota with her husband and two children. She holds an MFA in Writing for Children and Young Adults from Hamline University.

Ask The Author!
www.rem4students.com

My World of Science

HOT AND COLD

Angela Royston

Heinemannn Library
Chicago, Illinois

Designed by bigtop
Originated by Ambassador Litho
Printed and bound in Hong Kong/China

06 05 04 03 02
10 9 8 7 6 5 4 3 2 1

Library of Congress Cataloging-in-Publication Data
Royston, Angela.
  Hot and cold / Angela Royston.
      p. cm. -- (My world of science)
Includes bibliographical references and index.
  ISBN 1-58810-241-6 (lib. bdg.)   ISBN 1-4034-0040-7 (pbk. bdg.)
  1. Heat--Juvenile literature. 2. Cold--Juvenile literature. 3.
Temperature measurements--Juvenile literature. [1. Heat. 2. Cold. 3.
Temperature.] I. Title.
  QC256 .R69 2001
  536--dc21
                                     00-012870

Acknowledgments
The author and publishers are grateful to the following for permission to reproduce copyright material:

Ricardo Arias/Latin Stock, p. 22, Trevor Clifford, pp. 6, 10, 11, 12, 13, 15, 16, 17, 19, 20, 21, 23, 24, 25, 26, 27, 28, 29; Sylvia Greenland/Eye Ubiquitous, p. 7; Robert Harding, pp. 4, 8; H. Rogers/Trip, p. 18; Science Photo Library, p. 14, Stone, p. 5; Geoff Tompkinson, p. 9.

Cover photograph reproduced with permission of Images.

Every effort has been made to contact copyright holders of any material reproduced in this book.
Any omissions will be rectified in subsequent printings if notice is given to the publisher.

Some words are shown in bold, **like this.** You can find out what they mean by looking in the glossary.

Contents

Hot and Cold

Some things are hot. This baked potato is hot. When food is very hot, you can see **steam** rising from it. Be careful not to burn your mouth.

Some things are cold. Ice cream is very cold. As you lick the ice cream, it makes your lips and tongue cold too.

Danger!

Many things can be so hot that they can burn and hurt you. An oven may be very hot. What else in the picture will be very hot?

Keep away from hot things even when they are turned off. A hot iron smooths out wrinkles in clothes. It stays hot for a long time after it has been turned off.

Between Hot and Cold

Some things are not hot or cold. The water in a swimming pool is said to be cool, warm, or **lukewarm.**

This baby's bathwater is warmer than
the water in a swimming pool, but it is
probably cooler than your bathwater.

Temperature

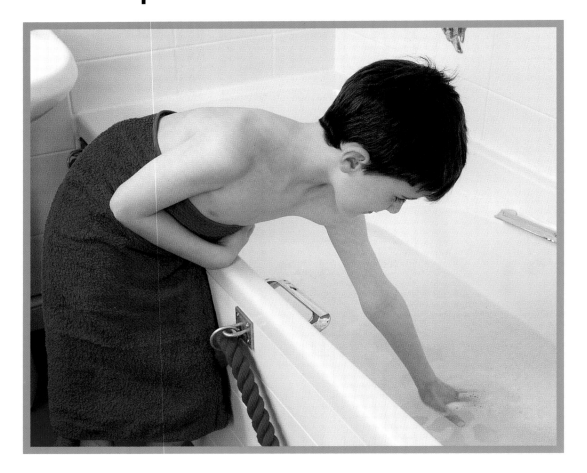

We use words like warm, cool, hot, and cold to talk about **temperature.** The boy is testing the temperature of the bathwater with his hand.

lukewarm water

Now they both put their hands in **lukewarm** water. The girl says it feels cool. The boy says it feels warm.

Thermometers

A **thermometer measures** exactly how hot or cold something is. This doctor is using a thermometer to measure the **temperature** of the girl's body.

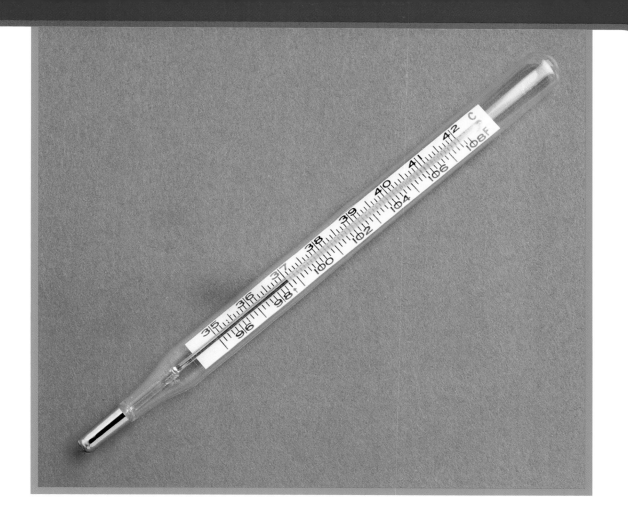

The end of the silver line shows the temperature. This person's temperature is normal at 98.6 degrees. When you are sick, your temperature can get hotter.

More Thermometers

This **thermometer measures** the **temperature** of the air in a room. It shows 68 degrees. The room is nice and warm.

This thermometer measures the
temperature of the air outside.
A temperature of 90 degrees is
very hot. 30 degrees is very cold.

Keeping Cool

In hot weather we dress to keep ourselves as cool as possible. Many people wear light, loose clothes. These protect them from the heat.

Wind can make you feel cooler. This girl is holding a fan that makes wind. The wind cools her down.

Keeping Warm

Hats, gloves, and coats keep you warm because they keep warm air near your skin. They keep cold air out.

Keeping warm air in and cold air out is called **insulation**. The curtains help to insulate the house from cold air that could come through the window.

Cooking

Food is cooked by making it hot. Some food, like this meat, must be cooked to make it safe to eat.

This girl is making a cake. She stirs the **ingredients** to make a sloppy mixture, or batter. When the batter is cooked in a hot oven, it turns solid.

Refrigerators

A refrigerator keeps food colder than the air in the room does. When food is stored in the cold refrigerator, it stays **fresh** longer.

The bottom part of a refrigerator is colder than the top. The freezer **compartment** is even colder. What is stored in the coldest part of this refrigerator?

Freezing

A freezer keeps food even colder than a refrigerator. You can keep food in the freezer longer than you can keep food in the refrigerator. Things get hard and cold when they freeze.

This boy is putting a tray of water into the freezer. The water will get colder. When it reaches 32 degrees, it will turn into ice cubes.

Melting

This boy is eating ice cream. As the cold ice cream becomes warmer, it starts to melt. It changes from **solid** spoonfuls into a runny **liquid.**

If you heat chocolate, it will start to melt. When the chocolate cools down, it becomes solid again.

Glossary

compartment small box

fresh good to eat, not old

ingredients different parts of a mixture

insulation material that keeps heat in and cold out

liquid something that is wet and takes the shape of its container. Water is a liquid.

lukewarm slightly warm

measure to find out how big, long, heavy, hot, or cold something is

solid something that has a size and shape. An ice cube is a solid.

steam tiny droplets of very hot water that float in the air

temperature how hot or cold something is

thermometer tool that tells you how hot or cold something is

More Books to Read

Baxter, Nicola. *Hot or Not?* Danbury, Conn.: Children's Press, 1995.

Burton, Margie, Cathy French, and Tammy Jones. *Heat.* Pelham, N.Y.: Benchmark Education Co., 1998.

Fowler, Allan. *Hot and Cold.* Danbury, Conn.: Children's Press, 1994.

Index